21 Verses
Backed By Science

DEEPEN YOUR FAITH

BY DAVID RIVES

BIBLE KNOWS BEST

21 Verses Backed By Science
...DEEPEN YOUR FAITH
by David Rives
(Bible Knows Best)

ISBN: 978-0-9857926-4-0
Printed in the United States of America
Fourth Printing, June 2020

DAVID RIVES MINISTRIES

DAVID RIVES MINISTRIES
P.O. BOX 2824 - LEWISBURG, TN 37091
Visit our website at www.davidrives.com

**Call 931-212-7990 for steeply discounted
bulk orders used for evangelism.**

email: booking@davidrives.com for interview requests.

TABLE OF CONTENTS

THE BIBLE KNOWS BEST

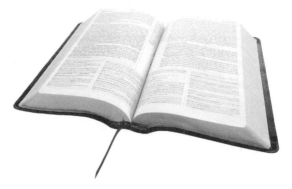

The Concept:

Even if you've never seen an episode of the TV series... Even if you never listened to the 1940's radio serial... Even if you are a millennial or younger, you've probably heard the phrase "Father Knows Best". It's an iconic part of America's culture, but more than that, it holds elementary truths that have stood the test of time.

But you see, I believe that the Bible is God's Word, and I believe that it was inspired by the Father Himself, Yahweh, the God of the Bible. So, if the Bible *is* inspired by the Father, and the Father knows best, then by association, the Bible also knows best!

Let me see if I can break it down a little bit further:

The **"Bible"** is God's Word of Truth.
"Knows" means "to have knowledge of."
And **"Best"** would indicate that it's superior over all the other options.

Basically, I'm saying that God's Word has superior knowledge. But if we look at the modern word "Science," we find that it comes from the Latin, meaning to "have knowledge."

In short, science *is* knowledge of the natural world. So when I say that the "Bible Knows Best," I'm also saying that when the Bible speaks on scientific principles, those scientific principles will stand the test of time.

In the same fashion, when the Bible speaks of history or prophecy, or anything else, I believe that it is always correct prophecy, true history, and accurate in whatever it's talking about. That's the whole concept of "Divine inspiration."

So, does the Bible Know Best? And has it stood the test of time? Absolutely! In areas where there seems to be some discrepancy in Scripture and Science, we must remember that science is constantly being revised, and consistently pointing to what the Bible already had stated. Whether it's the Earth hanging on nothing, with space all around, or the paths and currents of the sea, empirical science continues to confirm: The Bible Knows Best!

#1. Three Basic Universal Components:

Now, *very little* setup is needed to understand what we're going to be discussing. The Apostle Paul said "the invisible things of him from the creation of the world are clearly seen, being understood by the things that are made, even his eternal power and Godhead; so that they are without excuse." -Romans 1:20

He was stating to the Romans that we can *understand* God better by studying the things we observe around us.

Science is defined as: "Knowledge about, or study of, the natural world based on facts learned through experiments and observation." Science is confirming many of the things that we read in our Bibles. Science *is* knowledge of the natural world, and the Bible is *full* of knowledge.

Let's look at a simple verse - The first verse in the Bible, Genesis 1:1, the foundation of the entire Universe. It says *"In the beginning God created the Heaven and the Earth"*. But does the Bible Know Best?

Dr. Henry Morris once noted several interesting patterns within this verse: *"In the beginning"* is quite certainly referring to the origin of time. *"God created the Heaven"* describes the origin of space. *"...and the Earth"* is clearly made of matter.

In other words, the very origin of time, space, and matter seems to be alluded to in the first verse of Scripture! So, what is the origin of the Universe? It can be found in the *first verse*, and it doesn't start with random chance.

"By the word of the Lord were the heavens made; and all the host of them by the breath of His mouth. . . . For He spake, and it was done; He commanded, and it stood fast" -Psalm 33:6-9

#2. Chief Dust of the Earth:

Speaking on Wisdom, and its institution before time itself, Proverbs 8 says: *"I was set up from everlasting... While as yet he had not made the earth, nor the fields, nor the highest part of the dust of the world."* – Or, broken down in Hebrew, "the chief dust of the Earth."

An interesting side-note is that King Solomon, who the Bible's widely regarded as the wisest man on Earth, wrote this Proverb in the first-person as wisdom itself.

Now, what is the "Chief Dust of the Earth"?

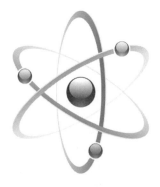

Well, at the time this was written, science hadn't yet discovered the atomic structure of everything that makes up the Universe. We now know that everything tangible that we see around us is comprised of atoms. A system of electrons, protons, and neutrons. But it wasn't until the 1980's that we could actually create the technology to visualize the tiny atom. If this is what the passage is referring to, I'll have to admit - the chief dust of the Earth is pretty impressive:

One single drop of water contains around 6 sextillion atoms! That's 2 sextillion Oxygen atoms and 4 sextillion Hydrogen atoms. A 6 with 21 zeros after it.

If Proverbs 8 refers to atoms, that means the Bible knew best and that King Solomon spoke of the particles that make up this world long before science caught up with Biblical Truth.

#3. Do Birds Fly By Our Wisdom?

In the book of Job, God asks the following question: *"Doth the hawk fly by thy wisdom, and stretch her wings toward the south?"* In Jeremiah 8, we read *"Yea, the stork in the heaven knoweth her appointed times."* It goes on to say that the turtledove, the crane, and the swallow also knows their appointed times.

Is this merely poetic, or does the Bible Know Best?

It's true, birds know when it's time to migrate, and typically, they follow the warmer weather south for winter, and back north as summer nears.

The Arctic Tern is a seabird, sometimes referred to as a "sea swallow." There are around 1 million arctic terns globally, and, just like other birds, they migrate. They take a particular course, often varying from year to year to take advantage of prevailing winds. They are known to mate for life, and have been known to live for up to 30 years.

But unlike other birds, their migration paths are quite extraordinary. You see, terns may begin their journey in Greenland, or the Netherlands, and pick a path southward, down the African coast... but they don't stop there. Some have been tracked to fly as far east as Australia, before they turn down and spend a good portion of the year in Antarctica.

As they begin their North migration, they will many times trace an entirely different route back, to end up in the far northern hemisphere once more. A 56,000 mile annual journey, equaling up to 1.5 million miles in their lifetime.

Do birds fly by our wisdom? Or does the remarkable Arctic Tern point to a much smarter Designer, who instilled the inherent knowledge of migration in the fowl of the air? The Bible Knows Best.

Luke 12:24 says *"How much more are ye better than the fowls?"* ...but does the Bible know best? Again, we're talking about birds here... simple creatures, right? Well, let's look at the smallest bird on earth, the hummingbird.

Even though they are the smallest of all warm-blooded creatures, they can still fly over 30 MPH, fly backward, and at birth, weigh less than a post-it note!

These amazing creatures flap their wings up to 80 times a SECOND, allowing them to hover over flowers filled with nectar.

They are able to determine sugar content, and they'll only consume nectar that is at least 10% sugar. Less than that could not sustain their super-fast metabolism, with their heartbeat of around 1,200 times a minute!

With this in mind, hummingbirds typically wouldn't be able to survive a long cold night. *However*, they "happen" to have a built-in mechanism called "Torpor" that goes into effect as they sleep, shutting down their metabolism to 1/15th the normal rate. It effectively slows down their heart rate from around 1,200 beats per minute... to 35! And the next morning, they wake right back up, ready for another day.

The tiny hummingbird has a two-step lung system that allows it to utilize all of the oxygen it breathes. This efficient design might not be necessary for life, but for a bird flapping its wings at up to 80 times a second, it certainly is a helpful feature!

The hummingbird can fly through trees or between branches at incredible speeds, but its eyes are on the sides of its head. How can it maintain the aeronautical ability that allows it to fly with such precision, without crashing into something?

Our eyes have one fovea, which allows us to focus in on one area while our peripheral vision is blurry. But that's not the case for these creatures. They have two foveae which allows them to see in-focus straight ahead and side to side simultaneously!

Their feathers grow-in as matched pairs, making sure they have an equal number on each side of their body. 10 primary feathers on each wing, and 10 tail feathers. It's pretty important for a hovering hummingbird to have equal lift. You wouldn't want a helicopter with an unbalanced rotor. But it seems this need is provided for. Chance? Or design by a loving Creator?

While hummingbirds are now only found in the New World, fossilized hummingbirds have been found in Europe that "supposedly" date back to the Oligocene epoch, *millions* of years ago.

Most interesting were the observations that beak, skeletal proportions, the shape of the tail, size of the creature, *and* the design of the wing all appear *very* similar to… modern living hummingbirds.

I believe that it's been about 4 thousand years since a select few

hummingbirds flew off of the ark, surviving the global deluge, and still today, these tiny creatures leave us in awe of their remarkable design, function, and flight.

While the Arctic Tern *certainly* holds the record, hummingbird migration can take these aeronautical acrobats several thousand miles round trip each year. One unique feature with hummingbird migration is that they don't travel in flocks, and they'll make the long trip *alone*, from some of the Northern States down to Central America, and back. But it isn't learned behavior. It seems to be inherent in the tiny creature. Their parents don't tell them the best possible route, or point them in the right direction, they simply move out at just the right time, no questions asked.

Most remarkable is the fact that banded hummingbirds have been tracked to find their way back to the *same* backyard the next spring. A feat that many commercial airline pilots have told me would be very difficult for a seasoned pilot to accomplish without modern mapping and technology.

In the Biblical book of Matthew, we read that our Heavenly Father feeds the birds of the air, and then, Jesus Christ, Yashua of Nazareth, goes on to ask: *"Are ye not much better than they?"* The fact is, while the hummingbird and the Arctic Tern is a truly incredible creature, with hundreds of design features that will leave you breathless, *we*, as humans, have been given superior reasoning and the mental capacity to study God's creation in more depth.

#4. Fearfully and Wonderfully Made:

So, let's turn now to the human body.

Psalms 139:14 says: *"I will praise thee; for I am fearfully and wonderfully made: marvellous are thy works; and that my soul knoweth right well."*

Does the Bible know best?

It is interesting to note that the most complex computer ever

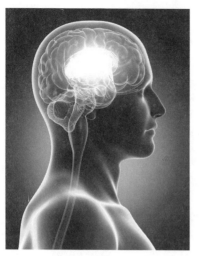

designed was built in only nine months.

That's right, I'm talking about the human brain. Over 100 billion neurons communicating with about 100 trillion cells in our bodies. To put this into perspective...

...IT IS MUCH MORE SOPHISTICATED THAN THE ENTIRE WORLD WIDE WEB.

In an age when we rely on digital devices for so much help, it's easy to overlook the astounding brain-power that we, as humans have. A device that is always with you that can not only solve problems, but can use logic, reasoning, creativity, and inherent instinct... A supercomputer! And there's a new one being formed every 4 seconds.

But the truth is, it takes intelligence to create technology like computers, satellites, skyscrapers, and moon rockets. And none of those are nearly as sophisticated as the design we find in each human being... for instance, in you. Why is it so easy for us to recognize that a space probe is carefully designed, yet so hard for some to admit that it takes a Designer (the God of the Bible) to make a creation as magnificent as the human brain?

The brain allows us to study complex mechanisms, including the CODE FOR LIFE! What's so fascinating, is that throughout the human body, we find extreme complexity but also interdependency. Let me illustrate with the simple mousetrap. Designed to perform a specific function, the mousetrap is only made of a few basic components.

You've got a wooden base, a lever, a spring, a thin metal hammer, and a catch. Definitely much simpler than, say, the eardrum, or the process of photosynthesis. But then again, the function of catching a mouse is a lot more basic as well. Now, were we to take away just *one* component of the mousetrap

(say, the spring), the design would fail to function.

Many researchers have called this concept "irreducible complexity." Think about it - Research in Biology is showing that many of the processes we see in the human body have complex functions, where every element must be present at the same time, in the correct order and position, or the mechanism fails to function.

This begs the question: how could any life forms have slowly evolved a complex feature or organ when all elements have to be there simultaneously to function in the desired way?

This can't be explained through gradual mutation or adaptation, which once again leaves us wondering how we could just "evolve" these features?

#5. Deoxyribonucleic Acid (DNA):

Let's look at Psalm 139: *"Thine eyes did see my substance, yet being unperfect; and in thy book all my members were written, which in continuance were fashioned, when as yet there was none of them."*

Does the Bible know best?

Deoxyribonucleic Acid, or DNA can be expressed as a *written* language that creates the blueprint that makes you who you are. Geneticists tell us that there are trillions upon trillions of combinations that make up human DNA, and your unique DNA was formed at the time of conception. You were your own human-being – not just from birth – from day one.

Your DNA Sequence, if written out, would fill up about 1,200 encyclopedia volumes! But if that's not impressive, get this: That same entire DNA sequence can be found in nearly every cell of your body. That means that there's enough information in you right now to fill every book in the Library of Congress. All 35 million books.

Everything about you is known by your Creator, the God of the Bible. His eyes saw your very substance before you were born, and nothing can be hidden from Him. You are fearfully and wonderfully made. Not just another animal in a long chain of death and evolution. A human being, made in the image of God, with a complex coded sequence. The Bible Knows Best!

#6. The Life of all Flesh:

In Leviticus 17:14 we read that *"the life of all flesh is the blood thereof."*

While the *majority* of animals contain blood, there are a few creatures that don't. The Sea Sponge would be a good example. However, the passage in Leviticus specifically speaks of the life of *flesh*. The sponge is an aquatic life form, containing no flesh. It's interesting to note that while optical effects cause our blood vessels to appear blue when seen through lightly pigmented skin, blood is typically red throughout the animal world, and it's always red in humans.

But does the Bible know best? Is the life of flesh really the blood?

Let's take a look at a fairly recent example.

Bloodletting was practiced all the way back in ancient Greece, but it was *common* practice as recently as colonial times.

The average adult body contains only around 160 or 170 ounces of blood, and it's estimated that over 125 ounces of blood was let from George Washington in the hours just before his death.

When we run out of blood, we run out of life! What might seem obvious now was looked at much differently less than 200 years ago. But the Bible knows best, and the key to healthy life was spelled out for us, thousands of years ago, in the inspired book of Leviticus.

#7. Don't Marry Kin?

Let's look at another example:

There are many instances in early Biblical history of people marrying closely related family. In fact, it doesn't seem to be a big deal, and if we take the Bible literally at its word, this would have been necessary just after Adam and Eve were expelled from the Garden, as well as immediately following the Genesis Flood.

But in Leviticus 18:6 things appear to have changed. It states *"None of you shall approach to any that is near of kin to him."* Some might ask: "Why now? Did God suddenly change His mind?" Does the Bible know best?

What we don't usually take into consideration is that Adam and Eve had a 100% pure genetic code. Beginning at the very next generation, copy errors would have been made in the DNA sequence, and over time, these errors would only worsen, producing non-beneficial genetic traits and mutations. Two people who are related will share a similar genetic make-up, in fact, it will identically overlap in some cases. But this means that any recessive genetic traits have a great chance of being exaggerated and passed on to their children, and the more this inbreeding takes place, the more birth defects, mutations, and even mental disabilities.

At the appropriate time in history, we were commanded not to marry close relatives, and long before genetic science, once again, the Bible knew best.

#8. Break the Pot!

Now, in Biblical times, Israel was given special instructions regarding the cleanliness of cookware that an animal had died in. Leviticus 11:33 says *"And every earthen vessel, whereinto any of them falleth, whatsoever is in it shall be unclean; and ye shall break it."*

The previous verse specifies that if it is clothing, or something you won't be eating out of, then it just needs to be washed. But why must the pottery be broken? Does the Bible know best?

Now, I've been to Israel about a dozen times, and during those trips, I've had the opportunity of examining a lot of pottery. Most of the pottery found in archaeological excavations is free of any glazing. Glazing is a secondary process that pottery has to go through to seal off the porous nature of the earthenware. Since this was not always common practice, many earthen vessels absorbed whatever they came in contact with.

This would include the bodily fluids of any dead thing that fell into the pot. Bacteria could then seep into the vessel, and any disease would be spread to those who ate from it. Thus the command to break it.

The truth is, germ theory wasn't even proposed until the 16th century, yet the scriptures seem to have again pre-dated modern science by thousands of years with incredible accuracy. Once more, we find that the Bible knows best.

#9. Got a Diesase? Get out of Camp:

Speaking in reference to those with certain diseases, Leviticus 13:46 says: *"All the days wherein the plague shall be in him he shall be defiled; he is unclean: he shall dwell alone; without the camp shall his habitation be."*

Does the Bible Know Best?

The first thing that you will notice is that he is being separated from the rest of the camp. This would have kept the disease from spreading. But before the 18th Century, much of the scientific community believed in the Miasma Theory, the idea that the Black Death and other diseases and plagues were caused by – wait for it... "Poisonous air."

To even further heighten the significance of what's being commanded in Leviticus, we also find references to bathing in running water. *Of course*, washing in still water is less efficient at washing away germs and microbes - But that knowledge is fairly recent within the scientific community.

You see, through scientific research and experimentation, Louis Pasteur pioneered Germ Theory... and it wasn't an easy journey. He was initially mocked, all the while, tens of thousands of people died from contamination in the operating room. It later became accepted science and a crucial step in the field of medicine and research. History tells us that Pasteur had a Biblically-based mindset, but whether or not he might have come across these passages in Leviticus we don't know.

Could God have been caring for His people by instructing them in good health practices thousands of years before we were to learn about germs? What do you think?

#10. Abiogenesis:

Genesis 1:27 says "God created man in his own image, in the image of God created he him; male and female created he them."

The anti-Biblical doctrine that life can originate from non-life, or spontaneously generate, has been pondered since the time of the ancient Greek philosophers. This abiogenesis was even suggested by Charles Darwin himself.

But, even here, the famed French microbiologist Louis Pasteur steps in with *real* science – not just philosophical ideas. He was contemporary with Darwin, and was publicly skeptical of some of Darwin's views on evolution.

Now, Pasteur, using scientific experimentation, was able to demonstrate that micro-organisms wouldn't grow in flasks containing boiled broths when dust and particles were prohibited from entering the flask. This effectively dispelled the idea of spontaneous generation.

Pasteur said "Never will the doctrine of spontaneous generation recover from the mortal blow of this simple experiment! No, there is now no circumstances known in which it could be

affirmed that microscopic beings come into the world without germs, without parents, similar to themselves."

Life does not create itself from nothing, and matter *cannot* burst into existence on its own. These phenomena have never been observed, and never will be, because there is only One who can *create* life.

He formed all living things

during the creation week, with amazing variety and design and Jesus himself stated: *"from the beginning of the creation God made them male and female."*

And, when it comes to the subject of biogenesis, the Bible knows best!

The more we look at life, the more we realize that we're fearfully and wonderfully made, not the result of random chance as Darwinian Evolution entails...

But, our culture is inundated with the idea that we're accidents – merely animals. That's what most public schools teach, that's the foundation of most college biology classes, and that's also what young children will learn in some of their favorite books. But the famous evangelist, Charles Spurgeon, said that one-day people would look upon evolution as being the most foolish notion to ever cross the human mind, and children would laugh at the concept. I agree – when you break it down into its core theories, the idea of Darwinian evolution really is ridiculous!

#11. A Spherical Earth, Hanging Upon Nothing:

Now, we've talked about *Biblical* accuracy when it comes to aspects of science, like animal biology and human biology, and we've seen how the cultural theories of the day were often way off base. A good example would be the flat earth. Many ancients believed that the Earth was a flat disk or plane, sort of propped up and resting on the backs of huge elephants, who stood on top of a massive turtle, who, in turn, floated in a giant pool of water.

Quite a fanciful story. It sounds like a fairy tale... But still quite a complex and detailed idea!

Job is often regarded as the oldest book in our Bible, although many claim that the Bible is only a fairy tale, containing no real science. We read in Job 26 that God hangs the Earth upon nothing... Not a turtle... not a flat disk... But a globe with space all around it!

Long before it was shown that the Earth is a spherical mass in the vacuum of space, we could have predicted it—if only we had paid attention to the Biblical account.

A giant turtle? Chance design? Or a Creator who hung the Earth in space, and commanded the stars of heaven to shine... Sounds like the Bible knows best!

Now, there's another myth, and this one has been perpetuated in modern day: Most of us who were educated about Columbus' voyage to the New World can usually recall a few basic details from our days in school.

Apart from the often repeated line "In fourteen hundred ninety-two, Columbus sailed the ocean blue," a majority might recall that Columbus wanted to prove the rest of the world wrong in assuming a flat Earth. But just a minute... is that bit of knowledge founded in reality?

A look at lunar eclipses enlightens us with the real history. Lunar eclipses occur when the Earth, Sun, and Moon align causing the Earth's shadow to block the light from the Moon.

The ancient Greeks observed this shadow, and Aristotle, living in the 300s BC, noted that, while some of his contemporaries believed in a flat Earth, lunar eclipses held one of the keys to showing its true shape. He said:

> *"Either then the earth is spherical or it is at least naturally spherical. ...The evidence of the senses further corroborates this. ...As it is, the shapes which the moon itself each month shows are of every kind straight, gibbous, and concave - but in eclipses the outline is always curved: and, since it is the interposition of the earth that makes the eclipse, the form of this line will be caused by the form of the earth's surface, which is therefore spherical."*

Yes, the spherical shape of the Earth was known long before

the time of Christopher Columbus' voyage. Around 2,000 years before, the prophet Isaiah referenced the design of Earth with the following preface: *"Have ye not known? have ye not heard? hath it not been told you from the beginning? have ye not understood from the foundations of the earth?"*
Or, to sum it up, Bible knows best.

#12. Dinosaurs and Behemoth:

Job 40 speaks of a massive creature that wandered the Earth in the past: *"Behold now behemoth, which I made with thee; he eateth grass as an ox. Lo now, his strength is in his loins, and his force is in the navel of his belly."*

Now, some Bible commentators in the past have related this creature to elephants or the hippopotamus, because, think about it, their large bodies do generate great strength. However, the commentators have been fairly criticized when you consider the context. Here's why: The passage goes on to say that the creature *"moves his tail like a cedar."* This definitely doesn't fit any of the proposed animals alive today, which begs the question:

Does the Bible know best?

Recently in Argentina, paleontological digs are revealing some of the most complete skeletons of creatures that we know today as sauropod dinosaurs. It's been plastered all over the news: Dreadnoughtus, the Titanosaurian Sauropod is being uncovered

in South America. This thing is *really* a giant, with an estimated length from head to tail of 85 feet. Think of that giant tail! Could that have been moved like a cedar tree?

I think it's interesting: The Bible told us about these creatures *before* paleontology uncovered them. So, *maybe* we should also trust the Bible when it tells us that they were created along with mankind, on day 6, in the beginning.

#13. Sea Dragons and Leviathan:

Isaiah 27:1 speaks of another dragon. This one lives in the sea, and he's called "Leviathan". In Job 41, we read a bit more detail: *"Canst thou draw out leviathan with an hook?... None is so fierce that dare stir him up... His breath kindleth coals, and a flame goeth out of his mouth."* However, with this last statement, a lot of people immediately dismiss the account. They say "That's fantasy. A fire-breathing dragon is only a fairy tale."

Is the Bible just a collection of myths? There's nothing close to this animal alive today. So, does the Bible know best? Before we delve deeper into Leviathan, let's look at another incredible creature - this one is not extinct - The Bombardier Beetle.

It has chambers inside its abdomen. Two of the chambers contain different chemical compounds. When the beetle is threatened, it releases these into a third chamber and mixes with a catalyst, causing a chemical reaction to take place and a scalding spray to eject towards the attacker. A chemical-shooting beetle!

But, let's think about this for a second: The beetle wouldn't have benefited at all from having just the compounds without the ejector system. It wouldn't have worked if the separating chambers were missing. It wouldn't have functioned if the catalyst was missing. In fact, you'd just

have a defenseless beetle. But all of the components are there in the correct order. That's irreducible complexity!

Two compounds, a catalyst, separating chambers, a firing mechanism and a directing nozzle. With some similar design components, leviathan may have only needed a few additional features: Perhaps some igniter system as flammable chemicals were expelled, and a fire-breathing dragon is not at all beyond the realm of possibility.

But possibility and reality are two different things. We haven't found Leviathan, so the Bible must be fallible, right?

Not long ago, I was working in the field on a dig, and we came across large, well-articulated fossil remains of giant fish, similar in appearance to the scissor-tail xyphactanus, and more importantly, what appeared to be portions of a Mosasaur skull! Yep, the giant sea creature that's been featured in famous movies like "Jurassic World" was real! The Mosasaur is thought to have been a marine predator, and some fossils have been found reaching lengths of more than 50 feet!

The Bible gives reference to a creature that might have been similar in appearance... Do you know where I'm going with this? Leviathan was described as a giant seafaring dragon, and was mentioned in Job, Psalms, and Isaiah. *"None is so fierce that dare stir him up..."* A creature so large and unapproachable that we're told *"upon earth there is not his like."*

Many large creatures, including many dragons, went extinct around the time of Noah's flood, and the Biblical record tells us that even the highest mountains were covered with water. This would explain why we see so many layers of sediment turned to stone preserving the fossils of millions of animals around the world.

#14. The Global Flood - A Catastrophic Event:

So, what *about* the flood? Was it real? Was it global? Let's look at the evidence:

Gen 7:19 says that at the time of Noah's flood, *"the waters prevailed exceedingly upon the earth; and all the high hills, that were under the whole heaven, were covered."*

It describes a catastrophe that destroyed almost all of the life on the planet. It involved tremendous amounts of water, and would have had an erosive power unlike anything that has happened since.

Does the Bible know best?

Catastrophism has been observed to form geological formations very quickly (some of them are even similar to what we see at the Grand Canyon).

In 1980, Mt. St. Helens erupted with tremendous force, and one of the side-effects was a natural dam of ash and debris that backed up Spirit Lake. In 1982 after a smaller eruption, a giant mudflow formed, washing out a huge new canyon in a matter of hours. Now, this on its *own* is significant, but the new canyon was *also* found to contain multiple layers of exposed strata. Soft strata layers, especially if the right mineral composition is present, have been observed to rapidly lithify... or harden... similar to the hard rock layers we find at the Grand Canyon today.

The Great Missoula Flood is another good example of rapid geology, and it's even accepted by *secular* geologists to be a recent catastrophic event that washed huge channels throughout the Pacific Northwest... and the destruction can still be seen today. It's not in the scope of this book to lay out the various theories on how the Grand Canyon formed, but these recent catastrophic events and the subsequent geologic formations should be more than enough reason for us to take a second look at rapid flood erosion... And certainly more than enough to call into question the supposed millions of years that are said to be necessary to produce massive wonders like the Grand Canyon.

The geological folding that's found all over the Earth is also an interesting study. Extreme folds and bends in the sedimentary strata aren't uncommon, and that can give us clues as to their origin. The first consideration is that many times, bends appear smooth along the fold. So, let's do an experiment. Take a thin strip of plywood. That's wood that has been layered together and hardened, and that will represent the strata, or layers of stone that are hardened. Grab it with both hands, and try to carefully fold it in half, just like the rock layers we saw in the photograph.

The first thing you may notice, depending on the thickness of the plywood, is that it is quite difficult to even *bend* the plywood because the individual layers are solidified into one solid piece.

The second thing you'll probably notice, is that when it *does* fold, it's NOT a smooth bend. If your plywood is anything like mine, it will fracture, break, and splinter when you try to fold it.

The same holds true for rock. Once the sedimentary strata has lithified (or turned to rock), it will not smoothly fold over. It's going to fracture as it bends.

The *only* evolutionary solution to this is to send the stratified layers perhaps a *mile* underneath the surface, so that it's heated and softened enough to bend. There's a huge problem with this theory, though, because at that depth and pressure, the rock would be transformed from sedimentary to metamorphic rock, *completely* altering the composition and appearance. So how do we get beautiful sharp bends in rock layers? You bend them before they turn to stone, while the sedimentary layers are still soft sediment and mud, under tremendous amounts of pressure, while the earth is very actively being shaped... Perhaps just after a catastrophic flood.

The effects of the global deluge in Noah's day, as recorded in the book of Genesis, can still be seen in geology today, in the form of "folded" rocks, bent not only under the effects of pressure or heat, but also hundreds of feet of strata folded while it all was still soft... sediment laid down rapidly in the catastrophic event of the flood.

So, it seems that geology confirms the flood account... Science is showing that the Bible Knows Best... but now let's look at another field of science...

Paleontology - Clams in Kansas:

In the past, I have had the unique opportunity to work on paleontological digs in western Kansas at a site classified as being part of the Niobrara Formation.

I didn't expect to find that, as I walked through the formations, I was literally stepping on thousands of fossilized clams, some in broken fragments, some with only half of the shell, and some were extremely large (around a foot in diameter)! But here's the most interesting thing: Some of the clams we're finding in the fossil record (not just in Kansas, but around the world) are preserved in their entirety, in a fully closed position.

When clams die, the muscles relax that hold the two shells together, and the clam opens. After a short while, that soft tissue and muscle disintegrates and the two halves break apart, and drift away. But that's not the case for some of the clams in Kansas (over 1,000 miles from the nearest ocean at 2,500 feet *above* sea level). So, what would preserve these specimens in the closed position?

A rapid catastrophe covering the clams with layer upon layer of sediment, mud, and soil would explain what's observed. But it would have to be a *lot* of mud. Clams can naturally burrow a short distance into the sand, and they can also easily work their way OUT. Some researchers have proposed that certain species of clams might even be able to escape through 8 feet of sediment! What catastrophe would suddenly bury these creatures with *more* than 8 feet of mud?

I can think of just such an event in the Biblical record. The account of Noah's flood in Genesis. The historical record states that the fountains of the great deep were opened, and hundreds of feet of sediment would have been stirred up, shifted, and re-deposited, burying millions of creatures around the globe.

As we'll see in a second, the same holds true for fossilized plant remains as well.

Giant Fossilized Trees:

While I was researching examples of flood geology, I heard about a particular fossilized tree in Northern Tennessee. After several weeks of trying to track it down, I was finally able to visit the site. The side of a mountain had been blasted away to uncover a coal seam, and what was discovered there was a very well preserved fossilized lycopod tree. This specimen was so pristine that in the 1970s, one issue of National Geographic featured photos of the tree in an article.

After traveling up to the area on a rainy day, it was apparent by the lack of civilization as we got closer to the site that this was a pretty remote area. Ruins of the old coal mining operation could be seen scattered along the hillside. A rough ride in a 4 wheel drive up to the end of the road, and then a long hike over streams and through brambles brought us to the site. There, perfectly preserved, was the massive fossil, and with it, many other fossilized examples of these trees.

Although similar to the modern horse-tail, these lycopod specimens are much larger than anything that currently exists. But there are a few features that make these very significant. Besides the excellent preservation, even down to the texture of the leaflet pods along the trunk, the first thing that stands out is the fact that these trees are fossilized in the *upright* position! The second and most significant feature is the fact that these trees can be seen extending through multiple layers of strata!

If a secular geologist saw the same layers of strata anywhere else, they would conclude that each layer was laid down slowly over time, taking several million years for what we see here to be laid down through gradual deposition, then lithified, or turned to stone.

But wait! How could a tree remain upright for millions of years while sediment slowly builds up around the trunk, preserving it from decay?

There is only one way to explain what is seen at this site and other similar sites all around the world… Catastrophism.

Even most secular geologists, and even atheists will admit that this has to be the case. A tree simply *cannot* stand upright for the amount of time suggested by evolutionary time-frames.

Of course, there was a catastrophic event that we read about in the Biblical record which would account for precisely what we find there in northern Tennessee. It would have uprooted vegetation, reshaped the continents, and buried a vast number of animals and plants extremely quickly underneath thousands of layers of sediment.

In some cases, root structure can be found, while in other specimens, it appears as if the trees might have been simply snapped off by force, again, fitting with the account of the flood.

The Age of the Earth - A Matter of Time:

We've spent the last few moments focusing specifically on scientific evidences confirming the Great Deluge of Noah's day, because this catastrophic event is key to understanding much of the Geological and Paleontological world around us. Let me see if I can sum up why there is so much controversy concerning the age of the earth: Because we see river beds eroding at slow rates today, and we see very few animals being preserved as fossils today, evolution interprets this observation from an uniformitarianist's perspective. This is the idea that the present is the key to the past. In other words, they take current values of erosion and fossilization, and extrapolate back into the past at the same slow rate. This certainly would give the *appearance* of an earth that is millions of years old. I mean, on the surface that seems like a pretty fair scientific approach.

However, these calculations are ignoring one *extremely* important historical event. You know which one I'm talking about! In fact, this event is recorded in hundreds of cultures around the world, and many of the flood legends have very similar themes. But one account gives not just *more* detail - but detail that is typically found in *history* books. That's the one we find in Genesis 6 through 8. As opposed to fairy-tales and legends, which are usually very generic, lacking in detail, the Biblical account is full of specific detail. The exact dimensions of the ark, the age of Noah when he entered, the number of days it rained, the height of the waters, the time before the floodwaters abated, the month, even the *day* of the month when the flood started! This is a real event being described. And it's a real event that *seriously* alters uniformitarian dating methods. We've seen that small scale catastrophes like earthquakes, volcanic eruptions, and floods can quickly create geologic formations that would have normally taken thousands if not millions of years, based on the slow erosion rates of today. If those small-scale catastrophes can have such profound effect on the geologic record, then imagine the effects of the global Deluge!

So, a scientist might take the historical record of the flood, and make a series of scientific predictions: We would expect to find layer after layer of sediment, or water-lain strata, stacked on top of each other. We would expect millions of animals to have drowned and been covered in the soft mud. We would expect many of those animals to have been preserved as the layers of mud were compressed under tremendous amounts of water. We might expect that some of the organic material buried in between layers would create organic coal and oil deposits. We would expect to see massive mountain ranges pushed up as the still-pliable layers were shifting. We would expect to find indications of past volcanic activity throughout large areas. We would expect there to be a genetic bottleneck at the time of the flood. We would expect a wide variety of species to be culled to extinction or near extinction around the time of the flood. We might expect new sets of adapted species migrating to certain regions and thriving. We might expect an ice age perpetuated by weather patterns immediately following the flood. We would expect to find evidence of people-groups with very primitive needs taking to caves for warmth in the years following the flood. We would expect a global human population consistent with extrapolations from the date of the flood... Should I go on? In fact, there are tons of predictions we can make based on the Biblical account of the flood... And what we would expect is *exactly* what we find!!!

The flood upends the entire evolutionary doctrine of eons and long ages, because it would have caused the very effects on the natural world that we see when we use the sciences to observe nature. What I'm saying is that modern science is again showing us that THE BIBLE KNOWS BEST!

Let's move on from the flood now, but continue with our theme of looking for patterns of Biblical accuracy.

#15. Underwater Mountains:

Do you remember the story about Jonah and the great fish? Jonah was commanded to travel to Nineveh to witness and warn the people of their wickedness. He attempted to escape from the presence of the Lord by boarding a boat, and after being thrown overboard during a dangerous storm, he was swallowed by a great fish.

Jonah states in his account *"The waters compassed me about, even to the soul: the depth closed me round about... I went down to the bottoms of the mountains"*

Now, Jonah was supposedly in the belly of the fish - How could he visually explain what was down there? Surely Jonah's account is mere poetry - or is there truth in his account? Does the Bible Know Best?

There are underwater mountains and ridges in the oceans. The massive ones are called "mid-oceanic ridges", which were first charted in the 1950s, thousands of years after Jonah's report that there were mountains underwater. More localized, and more in line with Jonah's journeys, the Mediterranean and surrounding areas are full of underwater mountains. We can see these on nautical charts and topographical displays, because they've been recorded in modern day. The mountains and elevations of underwater features are *now* well-known, but even so, there were no submarines in B.C. Israel. Perhaps Jonah's account of mountains in the depths of the sea was not poetry or allegory, but inspired truth, found in the Word of God.

#16. A Natural Process...:

To start with, I'm just going to throw out a few verses here, and I want you to pay close attention to the phrasing and pattern. You tell me what these verses might be referring to.

Job 36 says: *"Behold, God is great, and we know him not, neither can the number of his years be searched out. For he maketh small the drops of water: they pour down rain according to the vapour thereof: Which the clouds do drop and distil upon man abundantly."*

Amos 9:6 *"He that calleth for the waters of the sea, and poureth them out upon the face of the earth: The LORD is his name."*

Ecclesiastes 1:7 *"All the rivers run into the sea; yet the sea is not full; unto the place from whence the rivers come, thither they return again."*

Job 37:16 *"Dost thou know the balancings of the clouds, the wondrous works of him which is perfect in knowledge?"*

Do you see the pattern emerging? What is the Bible referring to here? If you guessed "hydrologic cycle," you are not alone. In fact, there are actually multiple references to the natural water cycle spread out through at least 3 different books of the Bible.

Ancient Greeks studied the natural world, and brought about many scientific principles. However, when things couldn't be explained naturally, they many times would make wild guesses. To explain the origin of life, Greek philosophers and thinkers settled for spontaneous generation... life from non-life. They also didn't think that rain was sufficient to keep rivers and springs fed. While it's certainly not the *only* source for the water, the hydrologic cycle is very important to agriculture, natural plant life, and for human survival.

In 350 B.C. Aristotle proposed this: *"The finest and sweetest water is every day carried up and is dissolved into vapour and rises to the upper region, where it is condensed again by the cold and so returns to the earth."*

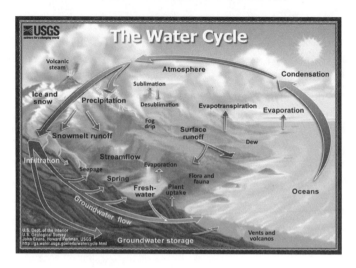

Predating Aristotle by hundreds of years, again, we read in the book of Job: *"He maketh small the drops of water: they pour down rain according to the vapour thereof: Which the clouds do drop and distil upon man abundantly."*

Notice the similar phrasing and description. Yet, Aristotle, in his attempt to attribute everything to nature has neglected to give glory to the Designer of the Hydrologic Cycle. We find, once again, that the Bible Knows Best.

#17. Springs in the Deep:

Did God foretell of another wonder in the natural world that could *only* have been known by Divine insight? In Job 38:16, the Creator asks Job *"Hast thou entered into the springs of the sea? or hast thou walked in the search of the depth?"*

In modern times, we have charted the depths of the seas very accurately, but this took scientific ingenuity and extensive exploration. Certainly Job had never walked on the bottom of the oceans. But we now know that there are hot springs (or hydrothermal vents) in the deep sea that actually contain diverse life.

So, how was an ancient writer able to predict this? Could simple men just have written a collection of stories with such accuracy? Or did the God of Abraham, Yahweh, actually speak to man, giving him insight into the sciences? It certainly seems more than coincidental that we would read about "springs in the deep," only to later discover "springs in the deep."

Actually, even this has been stripped of God, with some biologists proposing that these hydrothermal vents are where life originated spontaneously, and began their upward evolutionary climb to complexity.

We're warned that there *would* be those who worshiped created things more than their Creator. Romans 1:22 says *"Professing themselves to be wise, they became fools."*

#18. The Paths of the Sea:

One of the most incredible accounts of Biblical discovery comes from a man by the name of Matthew Fontaine Maury, the "Pathfinder of the Seas."
His story goes something like this:

In the mid 1800's, Matthew became ill and was laid up in bed. So, one day, his daughter came in to keep him company and began to read from the book of Psalms: *"What is man, that thou art mindful of him? And the son of man that thou visitest him? For thou hast made him a little lower than the angels and hast crowned him with glory and honour. Thou madest him to have dominion over the works of thy hands; thou hast put all things under his feet ...sheep and oxen, yea, and the beast of the field; The fowl of the air, and the fish of the sea, and whatsoever passeth through the paths of the seas. O LORD our Lord, how excellent is thy name in all the earth!"*

As she read the last portion of Psalm 8, Matthew sat up in bed, and began to repeat "Paths of the sea, paths of the sea..." He exclaimed "If I ever get out of this bed, I'll find out what these paths are!"

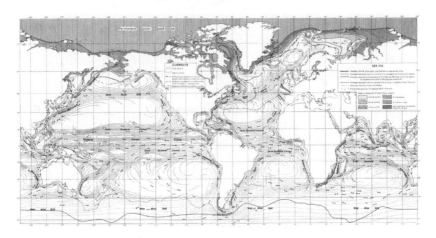

So – Does the Bible Know Best? Was there science in that simple verse, just waiting to be discovered?

Maury made it one of his life's efforts to chart the ocean currents and the paths of the sea, revealing extremely efficient channels for ships to follow. Channels that ships still use today. A monument in Virginia is inscribed in his honor: "Matthew Fontaine Maury, Pathfinder of the Seas, the genius who first snatched from the oceans and atmosphere the secret of their laws. His inspiration, Holy Writ…" Or, I would say "Bible Knows Best"

#19. The Stretching of the Heavens:

Isaiah 40:22 says that God *"stretches out the heavens"* but until the early 1900's, that concept was pretty difficult to grasp. We just didn't know enough about cosmology, and Einstein hadn't yet formulated the "Fabric of Space-Time." You see, in 1912, there was an astronomer by the name of Vesto Slipher, who, using the Lowell Observatory telescopes in Flagstaff, was able to measure an apparent recession of spiral galaxies through Doppler shift. Now, he didn't realize the implications of his find, until others began to propose explanations for what he had observed.

What he saw could have been explained as the result of galaxies randomly flying away from us, but that didn't seem to be the most logical explanation. So, what could it be? An easy way

to visualize this in 2D is to think of the galaxies resting on the fabric of space, and then imagine someone standing at the corners of the fabric and pulling. As the fabric was stretched, the universe (and the galaxies inside of it) would *expand*. Now, science has shown that an expanding universe would explain what is observed. So, we may be on the right track. But again, with the uniformitarian assumptions that are used in science, it's easy to extrapolate backward and try to fit the universe into a tiny dot. That's exactly what they do. They assume that a Big Bang must have caused the expansion, and they put an arbitrary date on the event of 14 billion years. This is highly theoretical. In fact, troublesome problems within the theory, including the "horizon problem" cause them to create a rescuing device for their model, claiming that perhaps the universe hasn't always expanded at the same rate, and during the beginning of the universe, the heavens were rapidly stretched before settling down to the more linear, slow expansion that we see today.

I would agree with this! But I wouldn't agree that it magically and spontaneously took place 14 billion years ago. I mean, a random natural event forming the universe seems pretty unlikely. It certainly isn't scientifically observable. But if the Bible is the inspired word of God, and is full of good science, then what if God *really did* rapidly stretch the fabric of space in the beginning, before setting it on a sustaining linear path of expansion? It seems again that the Bible Knows Best.

Contrasting the Bible (Good Science) and Evolution:

WOW! So far, so good. We've seen dozens of examples of good science in the scriptures, but what about evolution? How does it stack up against the "good science" test?

Merriam Webster defines religion as: *"A cause, principle, or system of beliefs held to with ardor and faith"*

Evolutionists *believe* many things... They believe that there was a non-guided Big Bang 14 billion years ago. They believe that this proposed event caused the formation of all the stars and planets. They believe that humans evolved over millions of years from a chance mixture of all of the right elements.

However, the dictionary indicates that, to be a religion, these beliefs must be held to with faith. Isn't evolution FACT? Well, not *any* of those beliefs are fact. Good empirical science is observable and repeatable.

No one witnessed a big bang 14 billion years ago, and we haven't been able to duplicate anything like it through laboratory testing.

There have *never to date* been any confirmed observable reports of a star forming. This would take thousands or millions of years to actually document... It's highly theoretical, and it's believed by *faith*.

We have never been able to create life from non-life in the laboratory, despite millions upon millions of tests in the most favorable conditions possible. This is also a faith-based belief.

All of these beliefs take a lot of faith, and their proponents hold to them with ardor... What does that make evolution?

Let's Jump-Start Discovery:

Okay, so we've looked at dozens of examples of scientific knowledge described or predicted in the scriptures, thousands of years before science caught up. We've seen that in some cases, it was the study of the scriptures themselves that lead scientists to discover new aspects of the natural world. Matthew Fontaine Maury was inspired to chart the ocean's currents from a simple verse in the Psalms.

When God told the Israelites not to eat out of contaminated pots, or to wash their hands, or to separate diseased people from the rest of the camp, it wasn't a mindless restriction just to test the obedience of the people... it was firsthand knowledge predating the proposal of Germ Theory by millennia. If we had sincerely read the words of scripture, then we would have been better equipped to understand the natural world around us.

In short, what we've found is that the Bible Knows Best... every time! And this is not the end. Our journey shouldn't stop with *past* discoveries. If the Bible can be trusted, and holds the key to good scientific principles, then why can't WE use the Bible to jump-start the process of discovery? I'd like to encourage our scientists to form hypotheses based on scriptural knowledge, and then test and verify those hypotheses.

Good science, using the scientific method, is observable and repeatable, and the scientific principles found throughout the Bible have stood the test of time.

Our ministry uses observatory-class telescopes to take astrophotography, or photos of space. There's a pretty unique art to taking these accurate and detailed photographs. You've all seen NASA's beautiful pictures and, if you're like me, you've wondered if those photos are modified and edited. The first time you're able to look through a top-grade reflector or a triplet refractor, you realize that those galaxies and nebulae are really there, but it's not until you connect astronomical cameras and technology to the telescopes and take your first long-exposure photo that you really glimpse the spectacular

nature of what's out there. Over the past years, I've had the privilege of photographing some pretty amazing and rare things through telescopes. There was one thing that continually came to my mind as I saw these remarkable cosmic creations: **"The Heavens Declare the Glory of God."** My motto has remained consistent for over 13 years now, and it couldn't be more true today than when King David wrote those words thousands of years ago. I've been able to catch a photo of a meteor as it enters Earth's atmosphere, the 2012 transit of Venus across the face of the Sun (a rare event that will not happen again in our lifetime), the Total Eclipse of the Sun in 2017, an extremely rare supernova taking place in M51, and more. The cosmos is full of wonder, and we've only been able to scratch the surface of what's out there, waiting to be discovered.

Immensity of Space:

Now, early on in my studies of cosmology and cosmogony, I realized that we have a tendency to complicate the formulae when it comes to distant stars and galaxies. Professionally, we talk about Astronomical Units, Parsecs, and Light Years. But can the average person grasp the concept of an Astronomical Unit? Do we realize that a Light Year is the distance light might travel at the speed of 12 million miles a minute after an entire year? While a Parsec might be described as the parallax of one second of arc, this simplification doesn't really make it any easier to comprehend.

Einstein proposed his theories of General and Special Relativity, including the famous equation $E=mc2$. This in itself is quite complex, but I realized that if Einstein can have his theory of Relativity, then I could also come up with my own theory of relativity. I call it the Rives' Theory of Relativity! But with this, I'm trying to bring the concept of "distance to faraway stars and galaxies" into layman's terms, so let's take a look:

The Voyager 2 space probe is currently on its way out of our solar system traveling at the incredible speed of 40,000 miles per hour. That's pretty fast! So, the Rives Theory of Relativity states that "Relative to the speed of our fastest spacecraft, we can determine the time required to reach objects in the cosmos."

Instead of immediately jumping to the most far-away objects, why don't we begin with something that's actually really close? Say, our closest star outside the solar system? Proxima Centauri can be found in the Southern Hemisphere, not too far from the Southern Cross. It's a smaller star in the Alpha Centauri system, and it's estimated to be around 4.2 Light Years away, but there we go again! How can we comprehend a distance like 4.2 Light Years? Let's use the Rives Theory of Relativity, and take a ride on our fastest spacecraft, traveling at 40,000 miles per hour.

An incredible 70,000 years from now, we would *just* be arriving at the closest extra-solar star! Distant galaxies like the Whirlpool Galaxy, at over 20 million light years away, would take 500 billion years to even get *close*. This sort of puts it all into perspective. We realize that while we can view these objects through telescopes and we can photograph them in extraordinary detail with sophisticated technology, there are still many mysteries throughout the Universe that are truly hard to comprehend. The book of Job tells us that our Creator does *"great things past finding out,"* and He has done *"wonders without number."*

#20. Grandeur of the Cosmos:

When we talk about wonders *without number*, astronomy is a great place to look. Genesis 15:5 says *"Look now toward heaven, and tell the stars, if thou be able to number them."*

It's estimated that there are around 7 quintillion grains of sand on all the beaches and deserts of this planet. That's a 7 with 18 zeros after it... A lot of sand.

But, did you know that we've tried to count the number of stars in the observable Universe? Best estimates so far come to well over 10 sextillion! That means that for every grain of sand on Earth, there are over 1,000 stars in the sky. With technology advancing, and new and more powerful telescopes being developed, that number could drastically change in the near future. Some astronomers are already considering that the number *might* be 20 to 30 times greater!

At this point, all we can do is guess, but one thing is for certain, a number that big is hard to comprehend. I'm not surprised. After all, the book of Jeremiah says that "The host of heaven cannot be numbered."

The Hubble space telescope, Ultra-Deep field, took a photo of a tiny area in the sky. They pointed the telescope in between stars, to try to peer into the darkness and bring out any detail that might be there. The area they photographed was about the same size as you can see from a hollow coffee stirrer held at arm's length. That's pretty tiny! They accumulated light over 11 days. In other words, they got the equivalent of an 11-day exposure time! If there was anything to see in this dark space, *that* should bring out the detail! When they processed the photo, they saw TEN THOUSAND galaxies! Not stars - galaxies, each one containing several hundred billion stars!

When Jeremiah says that we can't even begin to number the stars, the Bible *clearly* Knows Best! But the book of Psalms tells us that GOD DOES know the number of stars and He calls them all by name!

#21. Every House is Built By Someone:

As we wrap up, I want to leave you with an analogy. Hebrews 3:4 states: *"For every house is builded by some man; but he that built all things is God."*

Let's say you're walking through the forest, and you happen onto a clearing. In this clearing is a beautiful rustic cabin. Perhaps one of the best you've ever seen. You immediately think to yourself "Wow, 10 million years ago, there must have been a violent storm that snapped off the surrounding trees, and they fell into an intricate pattern forming the walls of this cabin. And over the next 500 thousand years, sand must have

slowly built up around the walls and lightning struck the sand, forming the polished windows of this cabin. A windstorm blew the sand away, and knocked fresh vegetation down on top of the structure, creating the roof of this picturesque cabin. What an amazing formation!"

No, I can pretty confidently say that not one person in this world would ever propose such a ridiculous notion. It defies all logic and common sense. But human life, or photosynthesis, or even the structure of the tiny cell is infinitely more complex and well-designed than a cabin in the woods ever could be.

Just as it is completely obvious that "every house is built by some man…" then it should be even more plainly obvious that He who built ALL things in the natural world is God.

There is a scientific principle, known as the *Second Law of Thermodynamics* that tells us that everything is losing useable heat, energy, everything is decaying, falling apart, tending to disorder (entropy). Cabins don't build themselves. People build cabins, and then the structure starts to decay, get worse, and fall apart. 100 years later, we would find it remarkable if the cabin is still standing and livable. Similarly, this world is progressively falling apart, and would have already done so if not for the sustaining hand of God.

Conclusion and Relevance:

There is only one way that the Bible could have gotten all of these verses scientifically correct (especially considering that many of the verses were written thousands of years prior to modern scientific discovery)...that would be if God Himself Divinely Inspired the words that the authors would write. Most of the concepts we've covered were far beyond the knowledge of the day. It means that the Bible is more than a collection of books written by ancient shepherds, kings, and poets.

Again, The Bible Knows Best. The Bible is the Word of God. And God certainly knows best. He knew it all from the beginning, and He's given us the mental capacity to discover things through science that point back to Him.

And if the Bible is true, and the Bible *is indeed* the Word of God, then what does the book of John tell us about the Word? It says that the Word *created* the entire Universe. It says that the Word was made flesh and dwelt among men. That's right. It's talking about Jesus Christ, Yeshua of Nazareth, the Savior of all mankind. He was more than just man–He was God Himself manifest in flesh. He came to this Earth to live, die, and be raised again, wiping our sins away, and offering us the Holy Spirit to guide us, and an eternal plan of *SALVATION* that was patterned all the way back in the Garden of Eden.

That salvation can be summed up in a nutshell in Romans 10:9: If you will "...confess with thy mouth the Lord Jesus, and shalt believe in thine heart that God hath raised him from the dead, thou shalt be saved." Do you have a sincere heart? Do you realize that you are a sinner, in need of a Savior? Have you repented of your sins? Do you believe in your heart that Jesus died in payment for your sins and was raised again so that you could live? Shout it out now or just whisper it. He can hear you no matter how far away. Confess Him as your Savior and turn your life over to Him, to become part of His eternal family.

If you have just given your life to the Lord Jesus Christ, then welcome home! Give us a call or let us know how we can encourage you as you grow.

Maybe you're a Christian reading this. If so, I hope this has served as an incouraging faith-builder, helping you to become a more effective witness for Christ.

Maybe you are not a Christian. If that is the case, I hope that this has inspired you to trust in God's Word. If so, I would encourage you to refer to the last few paragraphs and consider putting your trust in Jesus. Reach out to a pastor or Christian friend and **IMPORTANT:** Read the rest of the Bible for yourself. Remember, men – even sincere Christian men – are still fallible humans who can end up pointing you in the wrong direction, but God's Word stands forever as truth.

In a world that for the most part shuns *"absolutes,"* I'd like to make a statement:

The Word of God is ABSOLUTELY true – from beginning to end.

I'm David Rives,
Keep looking up. Truly, the Heavens Declare the Glory of God.

ABOUT DAVID RIVES
– Author, Speaker, Researcher, TV Host

The Creator left a pattern of His fingerprints across each corner of the universe, found in every crevice on earth, and imprinted in every cell of our bodies. A pattern that David Rives has devoted his life to researching, revealing, and sharing… while declaring the glory of God through scientific study.

David's world travels and research has made him an in-demand speaker with an abundance of knowledge and his powerful and inspirational delivery makes learning about Bible history and science fun and easy for audiences of all ages. His weekly TV show "Creation in the 21st Century" airs to millions globally on TBN. He is a weekly news columnist on science and the Bible, and author of the books "Wonders Without Number" and "Bible Knows Best." Featured on the History Channel, DirecTV's NRB Network, WND, TBN, Dr. James Dobson's FamilyTalk, FaithLife, CBN, ETV, METV, and heard daily on radio, David's exciting life and world travels are documented on his ministries' Facebook page with hundreds of thousands of active followers.

With his energy and enthusiasm, David's number-one goal is to awe those he meets with the incredible accounts of discovery, Biblical accuracy, and science. He shows us that each person is "wonderfully made" with purpose – a biological miracle from our Designer. He has led dinosaur field trips, safaris to Africa, expeditions into the Grand Canyon, and shared the Gospel to millions along the way.

Call or email to schedule speaking engagements and interviews:
Phone: 931-212-7990
Email: Booking@DavidRives.com
Website: DavidRives.com

OUTREACHES OF DAVID RIVES MINISTRIES:

Our weekly educational and inspirational Faith-Builders e-newsletter will encourage you with articles, short videos, and more, absolutely free. If you want to start receiving those, just go to: **www.DavidRives.com** and sign up.

In 2013, David began hosting a weekly TV show called "Creation in the 21st Century" on TBN. If you have cable, there's over an 80% chance that our program is accessible in your channel lineup. He interviews different PhD scientists on some of the very topics we've been discussing today, and it's a highly visual program that breaks down REALLY complex scientific issues into really simple explanations. If you want to find the weekly schedule or watch any of the programs on-demand in High-Definition, just visit:
www.Creationinthe21stCentury.com

In 2014 we launched what is one of the fastest-growing creation websites in the world. It's called the Creation Club, and is a place for Biblical creationists to share and learn. With thousands of articles written by columnists from around the world, you'll find an answer to pretty much any question you could ask, related to science and the Bible.
www.TheCreationClub.com

In early 2015, we launched the first ever TV channel dedicated to Biblical science. It's called Genesis Science Network, and is available for free 24/7 through various outlets. Watch streaming online at **www.GenesisScienceNetwork.com**, or you can find the channel on Roku, FireTV, or on smartphones and tablets by visiting the website. We offer inspirational and informative programming that appeals to audiences of all ages. From technical dissertations delivered by PhD scientists, to fascinating and easy to understand shows and documentaries that parents can trust, you'll find it there, on Genesis Science Network.

We have the largest online store for related materials called The Creation Superstore. In addition to products that our ministry has produced, we also sell literally hundreds of books and DVDs on these topics. Right now, we have over 1,000 products and growing. It's perfect if you're looking for continuing education for yourself, science and nature documentaries that will leave you inspired, or curriculum and homeschool courses for your children. **www.CreationSuperstore.com**

We also have an active social media presence, so please join the hundreds of thousands of friends on our Facebook page **"David Rives Ministries"** for daily inspiration, and you can also follow us on Twitter, Instagram, and TikTok **@TheDavidRives** where we post breaking news and short videos.

In the Summer of 2016, we opened the **Wonders of Creation Center** in Lewisburg, Tennessee - complete with exhibits on Bible history, Biblical creation, science experiments, special events, presentations, star parties and more. Learn more at: **www.WondersOfCreation.org** and set up an appointment to visit by calling 931-212-7990

All of these ministry projects, in addition to our core ministry, have upkeep costs. We ask for your prayer and support as we boldly proclaim the Gospel and the glory of God through science. Hopefully this short book has been a blessing to you, and we hope that it has given you new enthusiasm for God's Enduring Word.

Lastly, we all need the encouragement of knowing that we aren't animals, the result of random chance over millions of years. We're wonderfully made, with purpose. **These books are excellent learning and witnessing tools. Please consider ordering these to share with friends, neighbors, and church members. We offer steep discounts when you order them in bulk.**

Order the video "21 Verses Backed By Science"
which is a complement to this book, containing powerful
visuals, demonstrations, and breathtaking video footage.

Phone: 931-212-7990
www.CreationSuperstore.com

READER'S NOTES: